Rising Above the Ashes

BIBLE STUDY

*Identifying Comfort in a Time of Grief
To Reignite Your Joy*

DORTHA HISE

**purposely
created**
PUBLISHING

Scriptures marked NIV are taken from the Holy Bible, *New International Version®*, NIV®. Copyright © 1973, 1978, 1984, 2011 by Biblica, Inc.™ All rights reserved.

Published by: Purposely Created Publishing Group™

Printed in the United States of America

ISBN: 0-692-34783-6
ISBN-13: 978-0-692-34783-6

Special discounts are available on bulk quantity purchases by book clubs, associations and special interest groups. For details email: Sales@PublishYourGift.com or call (866) 674-3340.

For more information, log onto
www.PublishYourGift.com

RISING ABOVE THE ASHES
BIBLE STUDY

Identifying Comfort in a Time of Grief
To Reignite Your Joy

❦

Each scripture in *Rising Above the Ashes: Reigniting Your Joy After Any Loss* was shared from a place of love and support to be of comfort. During my various times experiencing grief, I turned to one or more of the scriptures referenced in the book. This Bible study is designed to support you in digging deeper with your own experience, to flesh out all that you are going through and will continue to go through and grow through. Throughout this study, you will find places to jot down your own notes and reflections. I encourage you to:

- Take your time and work through each scripture at your own pace.

- Make notes and come back to any passages that you want to further investigate.

The scripture used throughout the book was from the New International Version of the Bible. Feel free to use whichever format of the Bible that you are comfortable with using.

Read Jeremiah 29:11.

What types of things are showing up in your life that are causing you to question the plans in your life?

_____

_____

_____

_____

_____

_____

Do you feel trusting of God, including the plans He has for your life (that also includes his timing)?

_____

_____

_____

_____

_____

_____

Read Genesis 50: 21-23.

What does this verse mean to you?

_____

_____

_____

_____

_____

_____

What point in this passage spoke to you the most?

_____

_____

_____

_____

_____

_____

Is there anything in this passage that surprised you?
If so, how were you surprised?

_____

_____

_____

_____

_____

_____

Read James 4:1-8.

What does this verse mean to you?

_____

_____

_____

_____

_____

_____

Is there anything in this passage that surprised you? If so, how were you surprised?

_____

_____

_____

_____

_____

_____

Are there truths in this passage that contradict ideas we hear in the world? If so, what are they?

_____

_____

_____

_____

_____

_____

Read Job 17:1-7.

What does this verse mean to you?

_____

_____

_____

_____

_____

_____

Are there truths in this passage that contradict ideas we hear in the world? If so, what are they?

_____

_____

_____

_____

_____

_____

Read Psalm 18:1-5.

What does this verse mean to you?

_____

_____

_____

_____

_____

_____

As you read the Psalm, did you feel the strength of God?

_____

_____

_____

_____

_____

_____

What did you notice coming up for you with regard to taking refuge in God?

_____

_____

_____

_____

_____

_____

What does the notion of "the cords of death entangled me" mean to you?

_____

_____

_____

_____

_____

_____

Read Matthew 5:1-4.

❦

What does this verse mean to you?

_____

_____

_____

_____

_____

_____

As you read the words "blessed are those who mourn,
for they will be comforted," were you comforted?

_____

_____

_____

_____

_____

_____

What do you think is the key message of this passage?

_____

_____

_____

_____

_____

_____

Read Revelation 21:4-5.

What does this verse mean to you?

_____

_____

_____

_____

_____

_____

Are there truths in this passage that contradict ideas we hear in the world? If so, what are they?

_____

_____

_____

_____

_____

_____

How can you apply this message to your life?

_____

_____

_____

_____

_____

_____

Read Ecclesiastes 1:12-18.

What does this verse mean to you?

_____

_____

_____

_____

_____

_____

Which part of this passage spoke to you the most?

_____

_____

_____

_____

_____

_____

How can you apply this message to your life?

_____

_____

_____

_____

_____

_____

Read Philippians 2:19-24.

What does this verse mean to you?

_____

_____

_____

_____

_____

_____

Is there anything in this passage that surprised you? If so, how were you surprised?

_____

_____

_____

_____

_____

_____

How can you apply this message to your life?

_____

_____

_____

_____

_____

_____

Read Isaiah 40:1-31.

What does this verse mean to you?

_____

_____

_____

_____

_____

_____

Do any of the truths of this passage written thousands of years ago apply today? If so, which ones? How do they apply?

_____

_____

_____

_____

_____

_____

What do you think is the key message from this passage?

_____

_____

_____

_____

_____

_____

Read Genesis 21:1-7.

What does this verse mean to you?

_____

_____

_____

_____

_____

_____

Is there something in this passage that surprised you? If
so, how were you surprised?

_____

_____

_____

_____

_____

_____

What did you learn from this passage?

_____

_____

_____

_____

_____

_____

Read Psalm 46:1-3.

What does this verse mean to you?

_____

_____

_____

_____

_____

_____

Which point in this passage spoke to you the most?

_____

_____

_____

_____

_____

_____

Why do you think God included this passage in the Bible? What's the point?

_____

_____

_____

_____

_____

_____

Read Exodus 7:14-23.

What does this verse mean to you?

_____

_____

_____

_____

_____

_____

Is there something in this passage that surprised you? If so, how were you surprised?

_____

_____

_____

_____

_____

_____

What did you learn from this passage?

_____

_____

_____

_____

_____

_____

How can you apply this message to your life?

_____

_____

_____

_____

_____

_____

Read 1 Thessalonians 4:13-18.

What does this verse mean to you?

_____

_____

_____

_____

_____

_____

Which point of this passage spoke to you the most?

_____

_____

_____

_____

_____

_____

Why do you think God included this passage in the Bible? What's the point?

_____

_____

_____

_____

_____

_____

Read Psalm 23:1-6.

What does this verse mean to you?

_____

_____

_____

_____

_____

_____

Which point of this passage spoke to you the most?

_____

_____

_____

_____

_____

_____

Is there something in this passage that surprised you?
If so, how were you surprised?

_____

_____

_____

_____

_____

_____

Conclusion

Finding comfort to move through your grief, identify
and REIGNITE your joy!

❦

What's one passage that encourages you from this
study? How does it encourage you?

_____

_____

_____

_____

_____

_____

_____

_____

_____

_____

_____

_____

What's one passage that inspires you from this study?
How does it inspire you?

_____

_____

_____

_____

_____

_____

_____

_____

_____

_____

_____

_____

_____

_____

_____

_____

_____

_____

What's one passage that challenges you to change?
How does it challenge you?

_____

_____

_____

_____

_____

_____

_____

_____

_____

_____

_____

_____

_____

_____

_____

_____

_____

In view of what you've read for this study, what changes do you think God would want you to make in attitude, words, or actions?

_____

_____

_____

_____

_____

_____

_____

_____

_____

_____

_____

_____

_____

_____

_____

_____

_____

How can you apply the message of this study
to your life?

_____

_____

_____

_____

_____

_____

_____

_____

_____

_____

_____

_____

_____

_____

_____

_____

Psalm 23
A Psalm of David (NIV)

1 The Lord is my shepherd, I lack nothing.
2 He makes me lie down in green pastures,
he leads me beside quiet waters,
3 he refreshes my soul.
He guides me along the right paths
for his name's sake.
4 Even though I walk
through the darkest valley, [a]
I will fear no evil,
for you are with me;
your rod and your staff,
they comfort me.
5 You prepare a table before me
in the presence of my enemies.
You anoint my head with oil;
my cup overflows.
6 Surely your goodness and love will follow me
all the days of my life,
and I will dwell in the house of the Lord
forever.

Footnote:
[a] Psalm 23:4 Or in the valley of the shadow of death

www.ingramcontent.com/pod-product-compliance
Lightning Source LLC
Chambersburg PA
CBHW071757020426
42331CB00008B/2315